Rosa Parks

Published in the United States of America by Cherry Lake Publishing
Ann Arbor, Michigan
www.cherrylakepublishing.com

Content Adviser: Ryan Emery Hughes, Doctoral Student, School of Education, University of Michigan
Reading Adviser: Marla Conn, ReadAbility, Inc.
Book Design: Jennifer Wahi
Illustrator: Jeff Bane

Photo Credits: © Dorothea Lange/Library of Congress, 5; © Esther Bubley/Library of Congress, 7; ©Lewis Wickes Hine, 9; © keantian/Shutterstock Images, 11; © Joseph Sohm/Shutterstock Images, 13; © Bettmann/CORBIS, 15, 22; © Warren K. Leffler/Library of Congress, 17; © Everett Historical/Shutterstock Images, 19, 23; © Neftali/Shutterstock Images, 21; Cover, 10, 14, 18, Jeff Bane; Various frames throughout, Shutterstock Images

Library of Congress Cataloging-in-Publication Data

Haldy, Emma E., author.
  Rosa Parks / by Emma E. Haldy ; illustrated by Jeff Bane.
    pages cm. -- (My itty-bitty bio)
  Includes bibliographical references and index.
  ISBN 978-1-63470-481-6 (hardcover) -- ISBN 978-1-63470-541-7 (pdf) -- ISBN 978-1-63470-601-8 (pbk.) -- ISBN 978-1-63470-661-2 (ebook)
  1. Parks, Rosa, 1913-2005--Juvenile literature. 2. African American women civil rights workers--Alabama--Montgomery--Biography--Juvenile literature. 3. African Americans--Alabama--Montgomery--Biography--Juvenile literature. 4. Civil rights workers--Alabama--Montgomery--Biography--Juvenile literature. 5. African Americans--Civil rights--Alabama--Montgomery--History--20th century--Juvenile literature. 6. Segregation in transportation--Alabama--Montgomery--History--20th century--Juvenile literature. 7. Montgomery (Ala.)--Race relations--Juvenile literature. 8. Montgomery (Ala.)--Biography--Juvenile literature. I. Bane, Jeff, 1957- illustrator. II. Title.
  F334.M753H35 2016
  323.092--dc23
  [B]
                        2015026081

Printed in the United States of America
Corporate Graphics

table of contents

About the author: Emma E. Haldy is a former librarian and a proud Michigander. She lives with her husband, Joe, and an ever-growing collection of books.

About the illustrator: Jeff Bane and his two business partners own a studio along the American River in Folsom, California, home of the 1849 Gold Rush. When Jeff's not sketching or illustrating for clients, he's either swimming or kayaking in the river to relax.

I was born in Alabama.

I was a small child. I was often sick.

My family was black. Whites and blacks lived separately. Blacks had to follow unfair rules.

My mother was a teacher.
She wanted me to go to school.

But she was sick. I had to take care of my family.

Why do you think my mother wanted me to go to school?

I married Raymond Parks. He was a barber.

He helped me finish school. I worked as a **seamstress**.

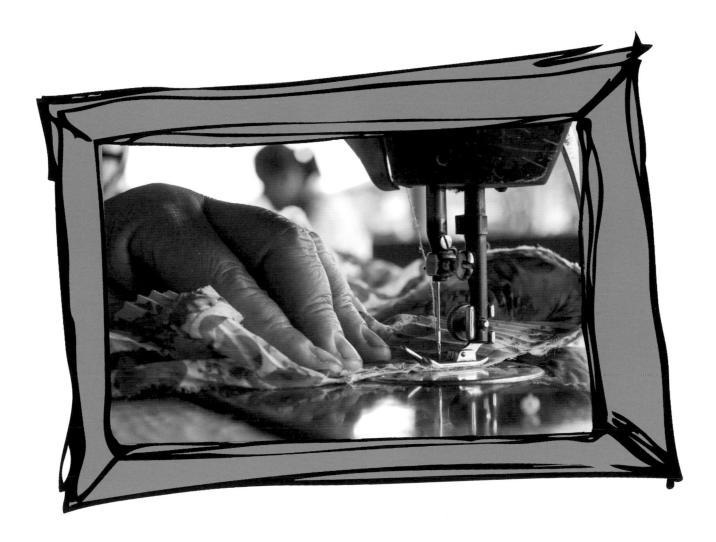

I rode the bus to work.
Whites sat in the front of the
bus. Blacks sat in the back.

I had to give up my seat if
a white person wanted it.

What is it like when you ride the bus?

One night, a white man wanted to take my seat. I was tired of **racism**. I refused to move.

I was arrested. I lost my job.

Black people were upset.
We decided not to use buses.

It was the start of the **civil rights movement**.

My story inspired people. They marched for **equality**.

Laws were passed. Blacks and whites had to be treated the same.

I moved to Detroit, Michigan.
I lived a quiet life. I died
peacefully.

I was a civil rights hero.
I helped end **segregation**.

What would you like to ask me?

1955

1900

Born
1913

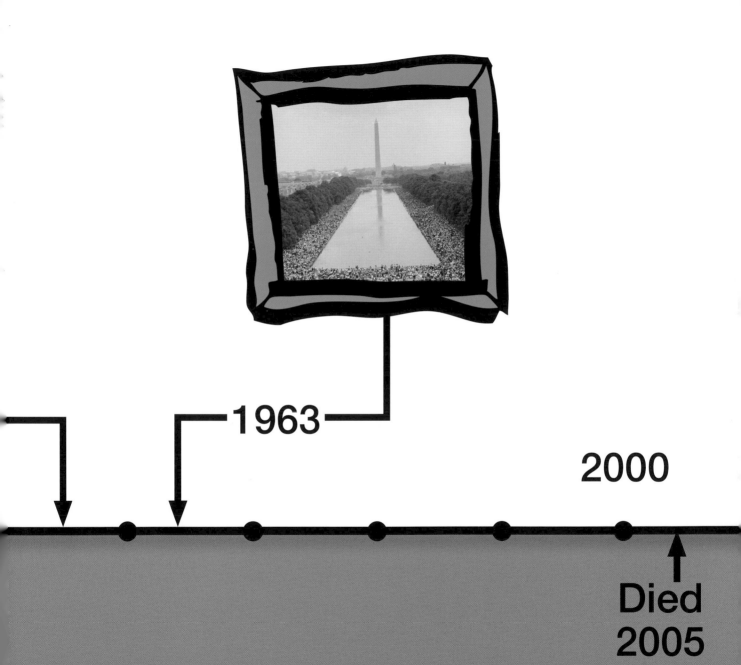

1963

2000

Died
2005

glossary

civil rights (SIV-uhl RITES) the rights that all citizens have under the law

equality (i-KWAH-li-tee) the right of everyone to be treated the same, without special advantages

movement (MOOV-muhnt) a group of people working towards a goal

racism (RAY-siz-uhm) the belief that one race is better than another

seamstress (SEEM-stris) a woman who sews for a living

segregation (seg-rih-GAY-shuhn) the act of keeping groups apart

index